NATURAL COLOURS

MEL WOODEND

NATURAL COLOURS

Copyright

Copyright © 2017 MEL WOODEND

All rights reserved. This book or any portion thereof may not be reproduced or used in any manner whatsoever without the express written permission of the publisher except for the use of brief quotations in a book review or scholarly journal.

First Printing: 2017

ISBN-10: 1546423524

ISBN-13: 978-1546423522

MEL WOODEND WRITING

UNITED KINGDOM

www.melwoodendwriting.com

DEDICATION

Natural Colours is dedicated to my husband Brent, my Mum Patricia and my Dad Michael – for always believing in me.

NATURAL COLOURS

CONTENTS

	Acknowledgements	Page 8
	Foreword	Page 9
	Part One - Air	Page 10
1	A Glimmer of Hope	Page 11
2	A Rainbow of Colours	Page 12
3	After the Rain	Page 13
4	Old Man	Page 14
5	Pink Moon	Page 16
6	The Lightshow	Page 18
7	Time	Page 21
8	You Are	Page 22
	Part Two - Earth	Page 24
9	An Unmistakably Autumn Day	Page 25
10	Autumn Leaves	Page 26
11	Bleak	Page 29
12	Canada Goose	Page 30
13	Crossing the Lines	Page 33
14	December Days	Page 35
15	Gardens in the Air	Page 36
16	Peacocks and Pigs	Page 38
17	Prince of the Ice Palace	Page 40

18	Scent of the Forest – The Evergreen Pine	Page 42
19	Senses	Page 44
20	The Forest – A Winter Walk	Page 46
21	The Snow Carpet	Page 48
22	The Wise Cat	Page 49
	Part Three – Fire	Page 52
23	Kitchen Colours	Page 53
24	Primal Colours	Page 55
25	Sun Dance	Page 57
	Part Four – Water	Page 58
26	Battered Senses	Page 59
27	Earth Rain	Page 61
28	Rain	Page 62
29	Rejuvenating	Page 63
30	Stalactite and Stalagmite	Page 64
	Previous Publications	Page 66
	Forthcoming Publications	Page 67
	About the Author	Page 68

ACKNOWLEDGEMENTS

I would like to thank my husband Brent and my Mum Patricia for their unconditional love, support and encouragement.

Thank you for always helping me to see in colour.

A big 'thank you' to my readers for supporting my work – I hope you enjoy *Natural Colours* and I hope you too feel mesmerised by the colours of nature all around us.

FOREWORD

This is my fourth collection of poetry – inspired by nature's limitless rainbow of colours and the many emotions evoked when we see and feel the natural colours all around us.

Does a visual colour evoke a certain sense? Or do our sensory perceptions automatically associate particular colours with personal feelings and experiences?

I believe colour can be many things – a sight, a perception, a feeling, a mood, a memory.

With this collection of poetry I invite the reader to explore the evocative power of the senses and the synaesthetic qualities of the colours we see and feel.

PART ONE

-

AIR

1 – A Glimmer of Hope

A glimmer of hope

Often shines

In the darkest

Of places.

2 – A Rainbow of Colours

Red is the sunset on a summer's night – the old saying of 'Shepherd's delight';

Orange is the fire burning in the sky – as the sun drops down turning to night.

Yellow is the blazing hot summer sun;

Green is the grass verge on my evening run.

Blue is the sky and the sea and the stream;

Indigo is the colour of midnight under pale moonbeam.

Violet is the heather on fell, mountain and moor;

A rainbow of colours each more beautiful than the one before.

3 – After the Rain

Rising

Arching.

Indigo, Violet, Blue, Green, Yellow, Red, Orange.

Nature's apology for a bleak downpour – a gift from the sun as it shines brightly once more.

Beauty travelling miles

Over rooftops, rivers, hills and seas.

Will the endless rainbow last forever endlessly?

4 – Old Man

Old man me

Watching o'er land and sea,

Tired eyes

With wrinkled lines.

Meandering through the endless sky

Watching from over mountains high,

My eyes your tears.

I see your fears.

I am not there but I am always here.

My eyes once shone bright

Now merely a light,

A candle in the dark.

Shining forever in your heart.

Bobbled jumper

Brown wood tobacco pipe,

The smell of summer - shirt sleeves rolled up.

Eyes crinkled in smile.

Let us lose ourselves in memories awhile.

5 – Pink Moon

ONCE ██████████

████████████████████████████
██████████████████████

██████ a ████████████████████
██████████
████████████████

██████ month, a full moon brightens █ Britain's skies.
████████████████ April's ██████ is the Pink Moon.
████████████████
████████████████████
████████████████████████
████
██████████████████████████████
████
████████████████████████████
████████████████████

The Pink Moon ████████████████
will not necessarily look pink.

But ████████████████ every year we see a Pink Moon

in April. ▮▮▮ moss pink ▮, ▮ wild ▮ phlox flower, ▮▮▮

▮▮▮ Full Sprouting Grass Moon, the Egg Moon ▮▮▮

▮▮▮

▮▮▮ ▮

▮▮▮

▮▮▮

▮▮▮
▮▮▮

▮▮▮ after ▮
▮▮▮

▮▮▮ the ▮▮▮ Easter ▮
▮▮▮

▮▮▮
▮▮▮ festival.

Griffiths, J. (2017) 'ONCE IN A BLUE MOON When is the Pink Moon in April 2017, what's special about this full moon and how often do they occur? April's orb has a special significance for the dates of religious events'

https://www.thesun.co.uk/living/3132873/pink-moon-april-2017/ (2017) Accessed 22/3/17.

6 – The Lightshow

Dark turning to light - mesmerising stripes and dashes and lines of light dancing across the sky…

> …Fighting, filtering their way in. Pummeling the dark like a pillow fight. The light wins and dances gleefully.

Cool morning light opens the world to human vision with shapes and outlines sculpted beautifully.

> Houses, buildings, factories standing tall - all clear and perfectly linear against the ever changing natural sky; like a child's silhouette of rooftops crafted carefully with pencil and ruler then cut out of the blackest sugar paper.

Pink morning light and thick white snow clouds puffy and full cast an eerie shroud.

> But the bright morning sun burns through.

Yellow and bright it fights away the eerie morning light and brings joy to the day like an oil lamp blazing and fiery the yellow sun pushes and pulls the clouds apart into cotton candy tufts…

> …Revealing a light blue sky cool and calming this winter's day. The blue twinkles through for a few hours and the yellow sun busily burns the twinkling diamond ice from pavements and

> playgrounds and frosty grass.

Squirrels dance and play and birds enjoy the merriment of the sunshine – warming their wings as they forage and flutter for winter food.

> Friendly gardeners have already thought of them and provided seeds and treats dangling temptingly in well-kept winter gardens.

Before long the blue begins to fade into a dullish grey - like a snowman melting – only lasting so long until another day when it may freeze and snow and be rejuvenated into life once more.

> The blue sky will return to twinkle its colourful joy - the colour of summer holiday skies and picnics in the park, long afternoons in beer gardens, reading in sunglasses on sun beds, riding bikes on sunny canal banks.

But now Christmas is coming. The light fades. The sun splits itself into stripes of oranges and reds and golden yellows - it will not go down without a fight!

> Then night bows its sleepy head over the land where shoppers rush to and fro like tiny worker ants. Busily bustling this way and that under the high street's twinkling Christmas lights.

Car headlights wind their way slowly, lazily as rush hour builds - like a million staring white eyes creeping carefully along the roads.

> Factory lights switch off and in a row of houses a dazzling array of lights suddenly blast into action – as cold dwellers arrive back from shops and work

> and school and take refuge in the warmth with
> Christmas decorations providing cheer.

After tea the world is alight with the colour of TV screens flashing all the colours of the rainbow as their little rectangles entertain and educate and amuse.

> Then darkness - until the morning light breaks
> through again.

7 – Time

Time –

Is black and white.

It's a fact.

There's no room for grey areas…

You're either early…

Or on time…

Or you're late.

Time –

Is black and white.

It's a fact.

Enjoy every minute…

You never know if it could be your last…

Because time is the everlasting concept…

That never lasts long enough.

8 – You Are

You are the red of sunset burning in the sky –

Brown Canada geese migrating, calling as they fly.

You are the cheerful face of the yellow daffodil bobbing in the breeze –

The shiny white ice lingering on a woven web, frozen in the winter freeze.

You are the grey taste of tears fresh from my eyes –

But the rainbow of reasons why, I should embrace life.

You are the teacher who taught me all I know –

Half of the people into whom, I have proudly grown.

You are the power of the deep blue sea as white surf crashes on the shore –

The wild purple heather blowing, straggly but surviving upon a dark green moor.

NATURAL COLOURS

You are the warm familiar scent of a green geranium leaf –

The brown eyed memory, still comforting in grief.

You are the joy of endless yellow summer days –

Of deep blue rock pools and spuddling, in a sandy sunny haze.

You are the pink blossoms of spring and fiery orange of an autumn tree –

The red blood and the inspiration, flowing through me.

You are the clear clean rain refreshing on a sultry summer's day –

The cosy chrysalism feeling, chasing the winter blues away.

You are always. You just are.

I know that you will never be too far.

PART TWO

-

EARTH

9 – An Unmistakably Autumn Day

Leaves of rich reds, russets, golds –

Hurtle swirling to the ground.

Autumn carpets brightly laid –

Crisp and crunching sound.

                              A chill in the air –

                              Grey morning fog.

                              Mists curl eerie and still –

                              Ghostly faces loom from the gloom
                              on their morning jog.

Pale sun fights to brighten the skies –

Burning fog and mist away.

Low sun sets in a reddening sky –

An unmistakably autumn day.

10 – Autumn Leaves

Floating,

Fluttering,

Crisp & dry.

Autumn leaves litter an angry sky.

Lying,

Dying,

On the ground.

October death scattered all around.

Whispering –

Quivering –

Voices in a hospital bay.

Shallow breathing till so still you lay.

On the breath when you stopped –

My heart stood still –

NATURAL COLOURS

Felt your life leave you.

Our hands entwined until…

Still warm & lifelike –

Face so soft & sweet –

A loving kiss goodbye till

One day again we'll meet…

Autumn doom,

Autumn gloom,

I hate the autumn days.

A lying sun tricking with its hopeful rays.

The world feels out of colour,

Cold fog hard slog,

The air so cold and dark and grey.

Trying to wade through every day

Knee deep in rusty autumn leaves and gloom,

Grey fog swirls revealing skeletons on the ground,

Red and orange.

Green and brown.

Life stopped coursing through their veins.

Leaves lie delicately brittle

Till the autumn rains come like floods of tears

Trying to wash away the pain.

But all in vain.

Pain red raw like blood pulses through my veins,

In peaks and troughs,

It washes high and low.

Under the orange autumn glow.

I can only see in monochrome,

Orange once so vibrant,

Now so sad.

Because I miss you Dad.

11 – Bleak

Blackened skies, scudding clouds and swooping gulls fill an ominous sky while

Lights glow dully in dark cottage rows.

Early evening light replaced by dark rain hammering

Against window panes blackened and depressed by relentless rain.

Kitchens provide sanctuary and solace from gloom - families snug round small tables eat and enjoy time together – away from the darkening day.

12 – Canada Goose

The goose from Canada sits in a cold wet puddle

In the middle of a grassy patch,

By the pavement,

In the centre of town.

It has found its way from marshes nearby.

It is out of place

Out of sync with its place in the world,

As it merrily wiggles its behind,

Leaving brown and white feathers behind.

The brown and white goose honks as passers-by stare

No one dares approach too closely,

They are wary,

Fearing a sharp peck from its sharp beak.

Unsteadily it stands and waddles away

This plump bird is not elegant,

A sitting duck sitting ungainly on the ground,

Until it flies away.

Once airborne the Canada goose soars

A silhouette of black against the reddening sky,

As it joins its gaggle,

A plump of geese flying in close harmony.

At one with each other –

With the wind –

With the sky.

We watch as they ride above

Rising on the wind,

Synchronised dancers of the sky,

Flying in formation.

Then distant –

As they travel far away –

Lost to the eye.

13 – Crossing the Lines

A fox

Crossing

Racing

Rushing

Chasing

Across the silver steel lines

To bushes beyond.

His brush

A swaying auburn flag

Glows golden in

The evening sun.

A fox

Crossing to safety

Safely across the lines

In silver moonlight.

Playing

Pouncing

Hidden safely

Across the lines.

In a clearing.

A fox

Crossing back to his den.

Eating

Sleeping.

Auburn coat wound

Into a coil

Curled tightly.

14 – December Days

I feel a chill when I wake up;

December is in the air.

Frosty ground crunching under a booted foot.

Walk carefully, don't rush –

Rushing, skidding on icy pavements is foolish.

Before you know it you'll slip and with a crick and a crack

You'll have a broken wrist or a twisted back.

December is short crisp cold days and sometimes rain.

Dark nights can feel so long so light the fire and snuggle in;

Close the curtains, seal the drafts.

Feel snug and cosy, warm, intact.

While away the hours with cosy conversation –

Loved ones round the table or watching TV.

The warmth is not just from the fire I feel it glowing within me.

15 – Gardens in the Air

Dress up the dreary concrete…

Create a colourful scent filled display.

Of pots and troughs jostling on the sunny balcony

High in the sky.

We share this garden in the air…

With the winds of heaven.

Calming, cooling, fortifying plants with air that feels fresher up here

Than in the gardens down below.

Hardy geraniums stand proud –

Stems sturdy and thick, withstanding of cold.

Pansies bob and sway –

A vast array of purple, pink and gold.

Roses climb, entwine –

Onto the balcony rail.

NATURAL COLOURS

Flower heads wise and fat and round, they sagely nod –

As they grow and climb and trail.

Snowdrops bob and dance –

Faces alight, merry and bright.

Heathers low to the ground flourish and bloom –

Lush dark green and pretty white in the pale winter's light.

Sheltered from the winter wind and rain –

By the balcony sides and the canopy above.

This garden in the air flowers and flourishes –

Full of bright winter flowers full of colour as they dance and celebrate the sun.

16 – Peacocks and Pigs

Walking one morning in a park far away

I can't remember the month – maybe April or May?

The park – a wild haven in the capital - far from streaming traffic and executive dreams.

Nearer to tranquil coy filled ponds, Japanese gardens and gentle splashing streams.

We round a corner past the manicured grass

A peacock sits atop a gate as bold as brass.

He glares accusingly, fluffs his long feathers of royal blue and emerald green.

Snootily looks down his pointed beak and begins to vigorously preen.

The peacock leaps from the gate with feathers gracefully aflow

Then stalks down the path and away he goes.

Walking further on through the park that day

I can't remember the month – maybe April or May?

NATURAL COLOURS

The park – a romantic haven for lovers holding hands.

Dreaming they are far away in exotic tropic lands.

We round a corner past the pink and red flower borders

Something strange is afoot there's something out of order.

I hear a squeal, a shuffling snuffling and an oink as we approach an earthy pen.

Surely not – a sounder of swine within.

Great brown pigs turning over the park ground

I never saw anything stranger than those pigs in a park - making the oinking sound!

17 – Prince of the Ice Palace

On a cold winter morning

The fat spider wobbles as he weaves and spins his finely threaded web.

I watch, transfixed with baited breath.

He carries on regardless,

Stoically ignoring the human head that bends and peers – watching every movement

In awe of

The intricacy of the details

Spun more quickly, more deftly than a human hand could ever achieve.

The spider

Holds me spellbound.

His prisoner.

As he sits prince like in his translucent ice palace,

Watching me carefully

With all eight eyes.

18 – Scent of the Forest – The Evergreen Pine

Looking up to the treetop canopy

I see....

Rising mist, swirling up from the ground.

Swirling and curling all around me to the

Orange, brown and yellow leaves - swaying gently on the trees.

A carpet soft but crunchy underfoot

Steals the silence.

Yet it is not quiet.

If I listen carefully

I hear....

Soft rustling as woodland mice and squirrels scurry to and fro.

Hidden from sight in the bushes low

Taking shelter under damp dark fallen branches.

NATURAL COLOURS

I breathe in and out. Steamy breath flows out and when I inhale

I taste....

Damp forest air cool and refreshing.

The fresh clean taste of oxygen

And icy rain on my tongue.

Closing my eyes standing still

I smell....

Woody bark and damp leaves.

This is the living scent of the trees

The evergreen pine growing tall and proud.

King of the forest.

19 – Senses

I see rain falling –

Glistening as clear as diamond dew drops in the sky.

Tears of happiness or sad dismay.

I hear the thunder rumble in the dark, dark night –

Waiting for daybreak.

A crackle and a flash of electric in the greyish pink dawn light.

I smell the earth –

Freshly washed on a wet summer's morning.

Drooping flowers on sentry duty in brightly regimented garden borders marking the start of a new day dawning.

I bend to pick a gentle sweet pea flower –

Rough edged leaves with fragile softly rounded petals.

Carefully cutting stalks to allow new blossoms to bloom.

I taste the air –

Cool, damp, fresh, salty from the blue - green sea.

Sweet from farmers crops in fields of yellow swaying in the dusty summer breeze.

20 – The Forest – A Winter Walk

In the cool shade of the trees, she drank in the scent of the forest.

Damp trees and wet grass mingled with the distant smell of wood smoke –

The rustling wind bent bushes into windswept shapes…

An artist's paint palette of wild lavender and heathers mixed in vibrant purple, violet, grape, aubergine, fuchsia and damson shades.

As she walked, wet leaves dripped cold droplets on her head –

and

down

her

neck…

She pulled her fleece collar tightly around her; glad of its warmth as the swirling fog mingled with mist rising eerily from the ground across the flat expanse of green and brown grass, moss and bracken bushes.

Passing a tall tree trunk its wood smoke scent caressing her nostrils, she lingered, reaching out to carefully touch its mighty bark –

NATURAL COLOURS

Young pink fingers trailing delicately over mottled brown aged wood…

Pausing by a gorse bush, she watched a spider busy weaving its web.

Seemingly draped with diamonds the spider glinted dazzlingly as dew drops formed against the back drop of bright white fog –

Fat in its blackness, the spider, with clever legs twitching worked elegantly unaware of her presence…

Feet warm in woollen socks and waterproof wellies she turned, hands thrust deep into fleece lined pockets, and she squelched on through the forest mud…

21 – The Snow Carpet

Thick and luscious like a carpet of white ice cream, gooey peak topped meringue –

Or a crushed ice summer smoothie…

The snow carpet twinkles under a bright winter sun.

Sparkling with a thousand tiny diamonds entwined in its fibres

The snow carpet invites sledgers and skiers to its smooth surface –

And children shouting and playing and throwing snowballs…

And dogs barking and prancing and chasing their tails…

And lovers lost in the glow of each other out for a romantic wintery walk.

Twinkling late into the day the snow carpet laughs joyously

For it has brought childlike pleasure and joy to so many –

Then it rests under a wintery sky black as the night…

But full of thick cotton wool white…

As more snow falls and the snow carpet is reborn, resmoothed, resurfaced.

22 – The Wise Cat

The wise cat has experienced life

She has age spots in

Her wisdom filled yellow orb eyes.

Whiskers of white

And the odd white fleck

Here and there in her jet black panther fur.

But the wise cat is

Good at disguises…

On a sunny windowsill her glossy fur as black as the night

Shines with radiant striped reddish tones in the bright sunlight…

She is

A tigress…

Swaggery & sultry

Thick tail

Swinging as she walks.

Or puffed up into

A fluffy tufty brush

When she plays or stalks.

The wise cat has velvet soft paws

Silky and smooth…

She keeps her sharp claws safely

Locked away…

Her sensitive pads so gentle

As she taps playfully at a toe…

Until the midnight hour

When werewolf like

She transforms.

From soft gentle pussycat

Blood is drawn

With knife blade claws.

The wise cat means no harm

She is just doing what cats do…

If I were an elegant graceful cat like she

Full of wild fierce beauty…

I know

I'd do it too…

PART THREE

-

FIRE

23 – Kitchen Colours

I smell the warmth of home

In my mother's kitchen.

Clean ironed red apron worn on rounded waist –

Loving hands carefully stirring a saucepan of something delicious.

I smell red peppers and tomatoes and green courgettes

As ratatouille simmers - occasional bubbles spit out of the surface - exploding into the air.

A Picasso of reds and greens splatter onto the fiery gas hob. It blackens quickly burning –

Turning liquid into solid.

Vegetable onto metal

Smells like coal charred on a fire.

Mum gets ready to cut soft white bread –

Crusts the colour of sand.

Middle white and light - fluffy like a cloud

To be sliced with sharp glinting silvery knife.

Metal on flour –

Then saturated with unsaturated fat.

Yellow margarine lubricates the clean white surface

Ready to be devoured by my hungry mouth.

24 – Primal Colours

RED

BLUE

YELLOW

Red is a vicious word – shooting sharply from poisoned tongue

Lashing, angrily like a dragon spitting hot red lava fire.

Red is love - passionate, hopeful, lingering love

Delicate as a flower as two lovers entwine.

Blue is ice – icy frozen arctic cold

When sharp frosts grip and squeeze their stranglehold over struggling seedlings planted too early by humans hopeful of warm spring days.

Blue is the tropical sea – sensual as it ebbs and flows its rhythmical pattern

Lazily, on hot summer days

Yellow is fear – fear of the unknown or of what we have known

Fear of reaction, rejection, loneliness, not coping.

Yellow is hope and faith – of long hot sunny summer days

Bright colours blazing in garden flower beds, ice cream, mustard on a barbecued hot dog, frothy cold gold lager to quench a hot dry thirst and sunflowers bobbing merrily overseeing the garden with rounded faces of joyful delight.

25 – Sun Dance

Silicon, oxygen, neon, nitrogen, magnesium, iron, hydrogen, helium, carbon

Ultra violet

Nebula

Dances

Across the sky –

Nurturing and

Colouring

Earth.

PART FOUR

-

WATER

26 – Battered Senses

Battered window –

Icy rain…

Cold and piercing through my veins.

Battered window –

Rain outside…

Hammering trying to break inside.

Sharp beating raindrops on the pane –

Sharp and beating…

Feel the pain.

Battered window –

From the rain…

Stand outside release the pain.

Drenched and drowning –

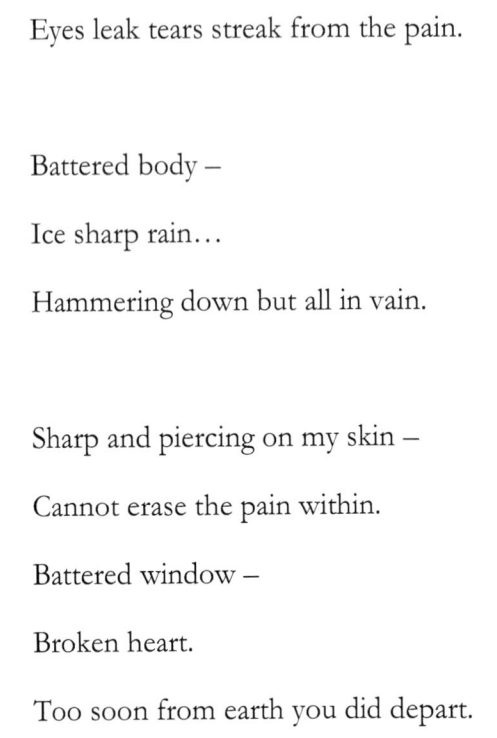

In the rain…

Eyes leak tears streak from the pain.

Battered body –

Ice sharp rain…

Hammering down but all in vain.

Sharp and piercing on my skin –

Cannot erase the pain within.

Battered window –

Broken heart.

Too soon from earth you did depart.

27 – Earth Rain

Let warm rain on a summer's day

Rinse your skin.

Smell the colours of the fresh washed earth

Brown and green and yellow and blue.

Let it heal you.

Let the colours envelop you

As you breathe them in.

28 – Rain

Trees shivering in rain –

Water cascading from tired arms.

Heads bowed in prayer –

Lining the riverbank.

Reflecting fragmented willowy shapes

Dark against the pattering pools of the rain splashed surface.

Fizzing and popping, splishing and sploshing diamonds of water

Falling like heavy jewels.

Swallowed into the depths and

Rushed down river by the current.

The rain becomes one with the river –

Eventually joining the sea.

My tired tears are falling –

And the rain becomes one with me.

29 – Rejuvenating

Clear waters weave between slippery rocks

Shining teasingly in their splendour.

Tempting man to try to step carefully on

To dangle feet in cool ice water.

Sunbathing like the kingfisher down river

Head tipped back.

Face lifted to receive the sunshine

Drinking beams of feel good warmth.

Rejuvenating him for another day

Like woodland animals harvesting for winter.

The sunshine keeps him going

From summer through a darkened winter.

Until

The spring sunshine awakens once more.

30 – Stalactite and Stalagmite

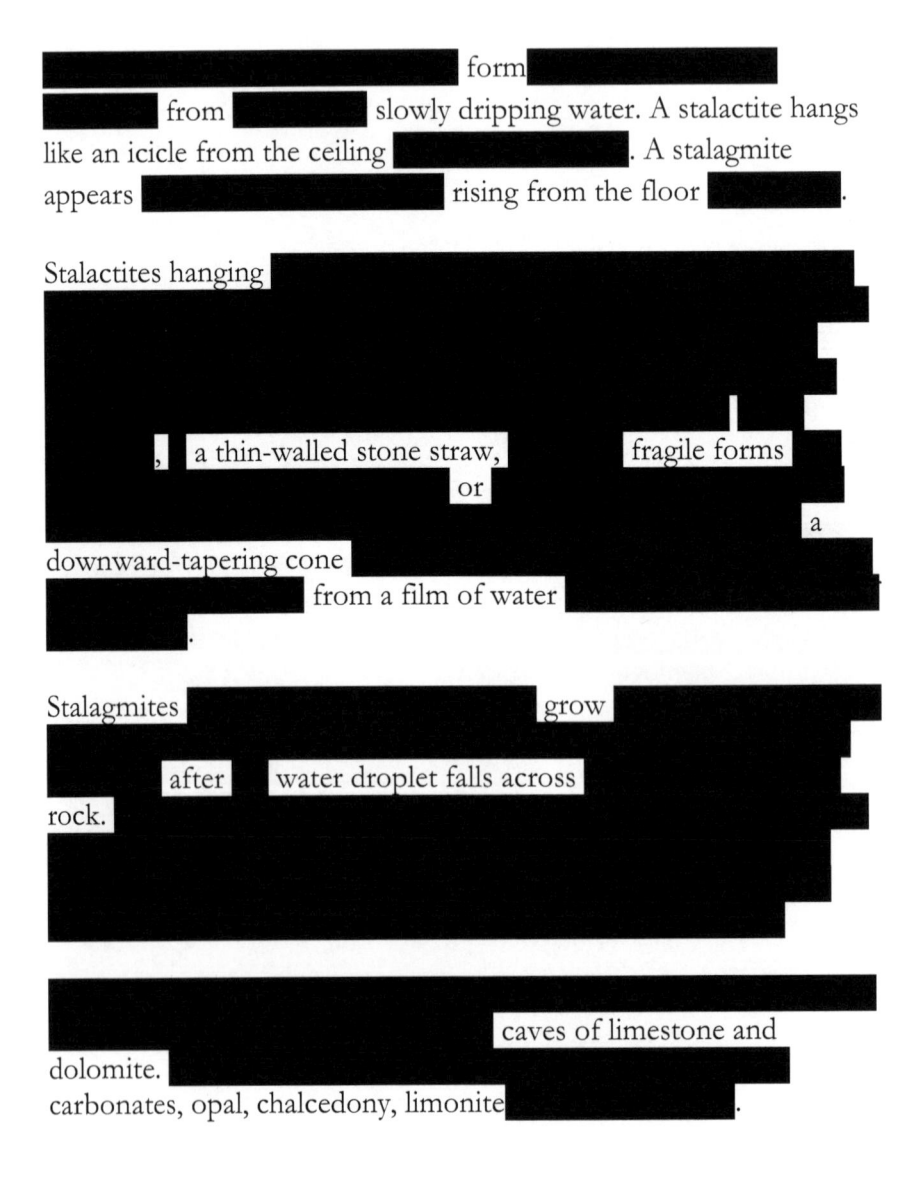

form from slowly dripping water. A stalactite hangs like an icicle from the ceiling. A stalagmite appears rising from the floor.

Stalactites hanging , a thin-walled stone straw, or fragile forms a downward-tapering cone from a film of water.

Stalagmites grow after water droplet falls across rock.

caves of limestone and dolomite. carbonates, opal, chalcedony, limonite.

'Stalactite and Stalagmite Mineral Formation' in Encyclopedia Britannica. https://www.britannica.com/science/stalactite (2008) Accessed 22/3/17.

PREVIOUS PUBLICATIONS

A Poet's Poems (2015)

Journeys & Memories (2015)

Poems Of Spring (2016)

All available from Amazon or from Mel Woodend at
www.melwoodendwriting.com

FORTHCOMING PUBLICATIONS

Mel is branching out from poetry into the genre of Children's Literature.

Please look out for her debut children's story *Tails of a Little Brown Mouse* – coming soon - as part of the *Brown Mouse* trilogy.

She will soon be turning her Blog *My Diary of a Cat Owner* into a novella.

ABOUT THE AUTHOR

Mel Woodend has written three previous poetry collections, including award winning poem 'Plight of the Turtles' - She is studying for an MA in Creative Writing and enjoys bodyboarding and blogging about her pet cat.

Please subscribe to her website for free at www.melwoodendwriting.com to receive a free mini poetry e book and updates of Mel's forthcoming publications and poetry events.

NATURAL COLOURS

MEL WOODEND

Printed in Great Britain
by Amazon